Seen

Dione Hoohauoli Fernandez

Made with ❤ on the BookLeaf Publishing Platform
www.bookleafpub.in
www.bookleafpub.com

Dedication

For those who feel invisible, you are seen.

Preface

In this world, overcrowded with noise and distraction, the simple act of being seen—truly seen—and understood is a rare and profound gift. These poems explore that quiet yet powerful yearning to be recognized in our most authentic form, to feel heard beyond the surface, and to find connection in a space where vulnerability is met with empathy. Each poem in this collection is a meditation on the delicate exchange between self and other, on the intimate dance of acknowledgment, and on the transformative power of being fully understood.

To be seen is not just to be noticed, but to be valued for our complexities, our flaws, and our silences. It is a recognition of our shared humanity, a bridge built from the deepest parts of ourselves. Through these verses, I invite you to look closely—not only at the words on the page, but at the truths and stories we all carry, often silently, within us.

Acknowledgements

I would like to extend my deepest gratitude to both the family I was born into and the family I was chosen into. To my birth family, thank you for the love, guidance, and foundation you provided me. Your unwavering support has shaped who I am today. To my chosen family, I am so thankful for your acceptance, kindness and understanding. You have been a source of strength and comfort that I didn't know I needed. Each of you has brought joy and meaning into my life, and I am honored to share this life with you.

And a special thank you to Liz, you were the first to encourage me to publish my poetry. I am forever grateful for your friendship and continuous support. Thank you for believing in me.

Chosen

All I've ever wanted
was for someone
to choose me
and to keep choosing me.
Even on my worst days
or better still
on their best.

No More

Don't tell me you love me
after choosing my oppressor.

Don't call me dramatic
when your idol threatens violence
for a different idea.

And don't confuse my silence
as acceptance of your hate.

You will no longer punish me as a child,
for I am a woman
full of life and fire
and rage.

So watch me burn
and take the patriarchy with me.

Unafraid

I am least afraid of the dark,
maybe.
Here I cannot see suffering
though I feel it,
a vacuum
stealing light where there is none.

Perhaps I am least afraid of the light.
Full of warmth,
mostly,
illuminating the destruction all around
till there is nothing left.

How about the dawn,
or dusk?
The in between.
A beginning
and an ending.
Here I am least afraid.
There is endless hope
and limitless possibilities.

Surrender

I woke to a heaviness surrounding me,
squeezing what little breath was left.
I have no more fight.
I want to welcome the end,
to surrender
to the crushing weight of this life.
Maybe then I will truly be free.

A Message to the World, Part 1

I don't know what I would say
I don't know what message I would broadcast
to each living room.
I'd like to tell everyone
that they are worthy of
understanding,
love,
justice,
peace.
Then the onslaught,
image after image of violence,
of destruction,
of suffering.
So much suffering.
People taking
without consequence
without pause.
Pause.

My Empire

The sun rises each morning
and I with it.
Tired,
worn,
empty from giving so much
and receiving too little.
I want to be the heir of my own empire
filled with grace,
and kindness,
and humility.
Where everyone wakes with the sun
restored,
refreshed,
renewed.
Including me, especially me.

Bad Temper

Fire
from the inside out
everywhere all at once.
Or was it a slow burn
that grew,
until it could not be contained?
I waited to cool
but all you brought was heat
and I continued to burn
till ash was all that was left.

Where I Want to Be

Anywhere
that I belong,
anywhere
that I can be free.
To breathe deeply,
air clean and crisp.
A mountain high above the clouds
casting a shadow
over land and
sea
far beyond the horizon.

My Brother

I heard your cries
or was it the lines on your face,
the pain captured in your eyes
that stopped me?
Does it matter
since I felt it all the same?
The breaking, shattering, tearing,
fill in the blank.
Words of your choosing for destruction.
Over and over
till my nerve endings were ablaze,
and now ash.
I am still here,
unmoving.
Waiting for time to pass,
not too quickly,
waiting for the pain to end.

A Message to the World, Part 2

They continue taking
never stopping to think
of the consequence,
never stopping to challenge
the hateful rhetoric.
How can I broadcast understanding?
Because I don't understand.
I don't want to understand.
I will never understand.

Lonely Bouquet

bold red
against a backdrop of beige
people walking by
speaking in hushed tones
stopping if only briefly
no one noticed
the bouquet of roses
sent as appreciation
a thank you
for saving a life

Enough

A simple greeting,
met with anger
and hostility.
So many questions
so much blame.
They say it is my job to know,
to find what's wrong,
and fix it.
Is it my fault?
There is so much blame for what I do,
or don't do,
wrapped up with who I am.
How can I continue with this work?
Every other thought is for another
and the rest
for others still.
No time,
no grace.
Just thoughts of others,
racing by,
or stuck on a loop.
Do better,
be better,
will I ever be enough?

Mothers

a large tree
maybe oak
maybe willow
maybe a fruit tree
with branches for shelter
leaves that hum along in the wind,
and roots that burrow deep,
part of the earth
sharing
giving
growing
quiet and still and unwavering

Change

The wind tells a story of change.
Unpredictable.
Sometimes soft, a feather light touch
a gentle reminder of its presence.
Then a force
bending, lifting, throwing
leaving only destruction.
When it stills, so quickly
it feels like an apology.
How can I greet the wind as friend,
not foe?
How can I greet the changes in me,
and in you?

A Wish

Freedom for bodies
many somebodies

To run
wind through their hair
sun-kissed

To jump
splish splash
puddle after puddle

To stand still
long enough
to count the stars

To choose their own love
To live in the glow of after

Waiting

You ever feel you are waiting
for your heart to break?
Not today
or even tomorrow,
but eventually.
You ever want to harden,
to hold others at arms length
to stop the break before it has a chance
to stop yourself from falling
to stop me
from loving you?

Her Betrayal

Her eyes are open,
looking,
but not seeing.
She is lost
somewhere inside.
Held captive,
a prisoner
betrayed by her body.
Everything in chaos.
She tries for words,
but there is only static.
Rocking, trembling
reaching for someone or something,
or nothing
Lights and alarms flash in the periphery;
movement all around,
then stillness
and
freedom.

A Message to the World, Part 3

I want to say everyone is worthy,
but a sourness fills my stomach,
and I am frustrated that I let someone,
many someone's,
poison my soul with bitterness.
I don't know what message I would broadcast
to every living room.
I don't want to be
in every living room.
I want to hide in my own,
long enough to change the bitter
into something sweet,
into something worth sharing.

Instructions for Life

Lean in
to your worth
your desires
your dreams

Lean in
to the present
to love
to life

Lean in
to our grief
our loss
our hope

Lean in
to me
and I will lean in to you

Finding Meaning

I imagine walking along the beach
Or sometimes through the forest
feeling,
sensing,
such vibrant colors.
A breeze touches my skin,
Bathed in the scent of the sea,
or the trees,
standing in stillness.
Observing life and knowing
I can choose,
more than existing.
I can imagine beyond the horizon,
above the treetops,
and into the clouds,
maybe even among the stars.
Perhaps that is the meaning of life,
appreciating what is,
while dreaming and
reaching for what could be.

The End.

The final words in a book.
Except these stories continue
in my imagination
or as I revisit those pages.
But life,
I cannot re-read this story.
It happens only once,
I think.
Except in my dreams
or with a memory.
A faded image of you holding me
and me still
loving you.